The Making of a Man of God

A Study in Paul's letters to Timothy

W. M. Henı

GW00721735

Contents

Quotations are taken from the *New International Version* unless otherwise stated.

GB ISBN 1 902859 21 9
US ISBN 1 880573 66 0

Printed in GB
First published in 2001

The Open Bible Trust
Bethany, Tresta,
Shetland, ZE2 9LT, GB.

Bible Search Publications Inc.
P. O. Box 18536,
West St. Paul, MN 55118, USA.

Introduction

In the New Testament we have two letters written by Paul to Timothy and it is generally believed that these were written late in Paul's life. In the first epistle Paul is at liberty, and the common view is that it was written after he was released from his first imprisonment in Rome, of which we read in Acts 28. The second epistle is thought to have been written from Rome during a second imprisonment, from which Paul was never released, suffering martyrdom at the hands of Nero.

The situation was that Paul had left Timothy in Ephesus (1 Timothy 1:3) to take care of the church there. Timothy was relatively young and inexperienced and needed all the help and advice he could get. Paul and Timothy were extremely close and Paul addresses him as *my son* in a number of places (e.g. 1 Timothy 1:18; 2 Timothy 1:2). But Paul also uses another phrase to describe Timothy. He calls him *Man of God*. This phrase occurs in several places in the Old Testament, but it is only used twice in the New Testament, and both times it is used of Timothy. The first occurrence is in 1 Timothy 6:10-12.

> For the love of money is a root of all kinds of evil. Some people, eager for money, have wandered from the faith and pierced themselves with many griefs. But you, *Man of God*, flee from all this, and pursue righteousness, godliness, faith, love, endurance and gentleness. Fight the good fight of the faith. Take hold of the eternal life to which you were called when you made your good confession in the presence of many witnesses.

This title is used again in 2 Timothy 3:16-17

> All Scripture is God-breathed and is useful for teaching, rebuking, correcting and training in righteousness, so that the *Man of God* may be thoroughly equipped for every good work.

These two passages indicate a number of characteristics of the *Man of God*, and it is interesting to note that these characteristics recur throughout the two epistles, as Paul instructs Timothy on how he should conduct himself in Ephesus.

Timothy was the leader of the church at Ephesus, and some of what is said in the epistles has primary application to his work in that role; e.g. the instruction to engage in public reading of the Scriptures, preaching and teaching (1 Timothy 4:13). However, it would be a mistake to infer that only those in positions of church leadership can be classed as *Men of God*. The characteristics that Paul applies to the *Man of God* in the epistles to Timothy have relevance beyond church leaders.

At the start of the twenty-first century, there are a number of similarities between our situation and that faced by Timothy two thousand years ago. For example, Timothy was in an environment of growing hostility to the truth of God, both from within the church and from outside; other threats, such as materialism (1 Timothy 6), self-absorption and religious personality cults (2 Timothy 3), also required to be faced. There is nothing new under the sun and these issues still disturb those who would be *men and women of God* today. Therefore the advice that Paul offers Timothy is equally applicable to us.

The characteristics of the *Man of God* indicated in these two passages are that he:

- flees from certain things (e.g. materialism in 1 Timothy 6) and pursues certain other things (e.g. righteousness, godliness, etc. in 1 Timothy 6);
- values and uses the Scriptures to equip him completely for every good work;
- fights the good fight of faith;
- takes hold of the eternal life to which he was called.

This study attempts to trace these four themes through the two letters to Timothy and to discuss the application of these attributes to our Christian walk and witness. The four themes emerge as follows:

1. There are certain ideas, practices and people that Timothy, the *Man of God*, must flee from, or avoid. And conversely there are others that he must pursue. And there are two aspects to this.

Firstly, as they affect his conduct and his lifestyle—ways of thinking and behaving—he must turn his back on, and ways of thinking and behaving he must follow.

Secondly, as they affect his doctrine—ideas he must not allow to have a place in his belief system—and ideas he must embrace.

2. The central place of the Scriptures is emphasised repeatedly in the epistles to Timothy. They are the sole arbiter in matters of doctrine. However, when we look at the ways in which the truth of God was revealed to Timothy, and the way by which he was equipped to discern the truth or otherwise of particular ideas, we find that there are two bases on which Timothy knew he could trust what he believed.

Firstly, the fact of whom he learned it from—the influence of older, wiser believers on the *Man of God*'s belief system. There was a strong oral tradition at the time, with Paul and others passing on the basics of the faith to Timothy, with the instruction that he was to preserve the truth taught, and then pass it on in his turn. In addition, Paul also reminds Timothy of a number of "trustworthy sayings", which would appear to be hymns, or parts of a catechism already known to him. These summed up Christian truth neatly, in a memorable way. Much of the basic, apostolic truth that Timothy held came to him from these sources.

Secondly, and perhaps more importantly, the foundation of what Timothy believed was Scripture. And again there is a great deal said about this—the place of Scripture in the faith framework of the *Man of God*.

3. Paul sees life for the *Man of God* not as a trouble-free existence, but as a war to be fought, and as a race to be run, requiring discipline, self-control and perseverance. The metaphors of the soldier and the athlete are used to illustrate this truth.

4. The *Man of God* is offered eternal life by the grace of God, through faith in Christ. Yet Paul urges Timothy to "take hold" of eternal life. The Christian is not asked to be passive, but to work hard at conducting himself in a manner consistent with the position to which God has raised him in Christ.

Paul was writing at a time when false doctrines and wrong teaching were mushrooming. Opposition was also growing, especially by the time 2 Timothy was written. So the call to the *Man of God* was to hold fast in the face of desertion from the truth, distortion of truth and opposition to the truth. The environment is not dissimilar to ours and the issues that are identified for the *Man of God* in these two letters are equally applicable to the *man* or *woman of God* living today.

Man of God

Flee - Pursue

If the *Man* or *Woman of God* is not to be diverted from the truth into wrong behaviour or incorrect beliefs he or she must keep away from corrupting influences. In the two letters to Timothy, there are six potential dangers that Paul identifies as pitfalls to be avoided. In each case, however, he suggests a positive alternative, and this approach helps us to see the issues more clearly.

1. Have nothing to do with godless myths

> Have nothing to do with godless myths and old wives' tales; rather, train yourself to be godly. (1 Timothy 4:7)

Here the positive and the negative are set side by side. The turning away from "worldly stories, fit only for credulous old women" (Weymouth) is set directly opposite training for godliness. What is meant by these two opposites?

In the early verses of chapter 4 Paul has warned Timothy about the work of deceiving spirits and things taught by demons (verse 1), and it is likely that he is referring back to these, although there were no doubt other aspects to these "worldly stories". He certainly attributes these "myths" to the work of Satan and, in verse 2, has a few uncomplimentary things to say about these teachers. But it is when we get to verse 3 that we see something of the content of their teaching.

They forbid people to marry and order them to abstain from certain foods, which God created to be received with thanksgiving by those who believe and who know the truth.

This is very severe teaching: rigorous physical discipline and the laying down of detailed rules. But in verse 3 Paul dismisses these practices as a rejection of God's creation. However, down the centuries this austere approach has proved very popular with religious people. If we have something tangible to do, especially if it is awkward, or involving effort, then we will feel that we have accomplished something and somehow built up 'merit' with God. But the reality is that they have no positive benefit at all. There is something in our fallen nature to which this approach is very appealing, but in fact it is impossible to put God in our debt. All we have from Him is given to us in grace.

But immediately Paul supplies the positive antidote. If Timothy is to avoid rigorous austerity, what should he turn to? Verse 7 says he should train himself to be godly. And this form of "training" is deliberately set in opposition to the futile disciplines of the heretics.

It is clear here that it is something to be worked at. It is something we have to be "trained in". Paul uses one of his favourite metaphors here, that of the Christian as an athlete running a race. Here in verse 8 he points out the limited value of physical training, compared with godliness, which brings benefits for the present life and for all eternity.

What, then, is "godliness"? The meaning comes into focus when we look at what Paul says about the inactivity of the conscience in the false teachers. In verse 2 Paul describes these teachers as, "hypocritical liars, whose consciences have been seared as with a hot iron". The conscience, having been seared, is inactive, which is disastrous because the conscience operates as the interface between our belief system and our behaviour patterns. An active conscience points out instances where our behaviour does not tally with our beliefs, and thereby enables us to live consistent lives. Towner (p103) points out that:

> For Paul the conscience is the faculty of decision. It enables the believer to proceed from the faith, the vertical dimension of belief and knowledge, to the corresponding horizontal activity of godly behaviour.

If the conscience does not operate in this way, then people will have no basis for proceeding from belief to practice, and are forced to fall back on strict rules, especially negative ones, which the religious mind has always done since time began. However, a clear and active conscience is a prerequisite to godliness. In the letters to Timothy, Paul mentions the need for a good conscience in his instructions to Timothy in 1 Timothy 1:5 and 19. He states it as a necessary attribute of a deacon in 1 Timothy 3:9, and he includes it as a feature of his own Christian experience in 2 Timothy 1:3. The central position of the active conscience in the life of the Christian means that godliness should be understood in terms of:

- the conformity of our thinking to the mind of Christ, and
- a consistency between our framework of belief and our behaviour - the vertical dimension of faith towards God and knowledge of His ways, and the horizontal dimension of our dealings with our fellow men.

The alternative to these "godless myths" that Paul sets out is training for godliness: working at increased conformity to the nature of Jesus Christ, in a genuine way, where our lifestyle echoes our beliefs in a consistent manner, with no contradictions between them. It is important to note Paul's emphasis on the need for *training*. Godliness is not something that is attained easily, or quickly. It requires application and development.

The pursuit of godliness also features in connection with the second danger that Timothy was commanded to avoid, the danger of materialism.

2. Flee from the love of money

In 1 Timothy 6, Paul warns Timothy of the pitfalls in the pursuit of wealth. Having described the temptations and traps which can lure men into ruin and destruction (verse 9), and the evils which follow from the love of money (verse 10), resulting in the abandonment of the faith, he emphatically sets out the contrast.

> *But you, Man of God*, flee from all this, and pursue righteousness, godliness, faith, love, endurance and gentleness. (Verse 11)

One of the errors made by those men of corrupt mind (verse 5) is the idea that godliness is a means of financial gain (verse 5). However, to Paul, the reality is very different.

> But godliness with contentment is great gain. For we brought nothing into the world, and we can take nothing out of it. But if we have food and clothing, we will be content with that. (Verses 6-8)

Contentment was an attitude that Paul had developed. In Philippians 4:11-13 he says:

I have *learned* to be content whatever the circumstances. I know what it is to be in need and I know what it is to have plenty. I have *learned* the secret of being content in any and every situation, whether well fed or hungry, whether living in plenty or in want.

Twice in these verses Paul emphasises the fact that this was a *learning* process. Like godliness itself, being content was something to be worked at, to be *trained in*, and to be *learned*. But the secret of contentment comes in verse 13: "I can do everything through him who gives me strength." What Paul is really saying in 1 Timothy is that total dependence on God means that he can hold material possessions very lightly. And when we think of the attitude of the Lord Jesus in this, we can see that it was consistent with what Paul is saying here; the Son of Man with nowhere to lay His head.

As far as Paul is concerned, his aim (and ours, too) is not that we should have *nothing*, but that what we have should be *enough*. And this is as hard a lesson for us to learn today, as it was for those of Paul's time. As in chapter 4, the source of error was false teachers, with whom the church at Ephesus was plagued.

If anyone teaches false doctrines and does not agree to the sound instruction of our Lord Jesus Christ, and to godly teaching, he is conceited and understands nothing. He has an unhealthy interest in controversies and quarrels about words that result in envy, strife, malicious talk, evil suspicions and constant friction between men of corrupt mind, who have been robbed of the truth and who think that godliness is a means to financial gain. (1 Timothy 6:3-5)

This is the negative to which "godliness with contentment" is the positive. The combination of conceit and self-importance, together with complete ignorance in verse 4, is deadly. But there is also the problem of a *morbid craving for arguments* (Guthrie p111), which results in all these negative relationships. And Paul goes on to describe these people in verse 5 as men whose "intellects are disordered" (Weymouth), who think that godliness is a means of financial gain.

Exactly what Paul means by that is not clear, whether they charged for their lectures or advice, or they had some sort of early 'prosperity gospel', is uncertain. But what is clear is that by this obsession with money, they had lost any sense of the true priorities of life. Godliness *is* a means of gain, for if it is linked with contentment it is *"great* gain". But this gain is not to be measured in financial terms. Instead it is to be measured in terms of the fulfilment that comes from leading a life that has real value, not just for the present, but for all eternity, and in terms of the reward to be granted by the Lord to all who persevere to the end.

Like Paul and Timothy, we live in a materialistic age, and moving constantly among people with such a limited outlook, there is a risk that we adopt the world's priorities and become preoccupied with wealth and consumer goods. It is extremely difficult today to function effectively as Christians in such a climate, especially in a business environment or any other situation where we are working as a team, or interact with others in some way. It is easy to be dragged into compromise situations, either because we fail to notice them, or because we convince ourselves that living in the 'real world' involves compromise, that Christian ideals do not work outside the church door. Unfortunately there are a number of Christians who seem to operate like this. The songs and sentiments expressed on Sundays, and the dialogue with other believers in Bible study groups, belong to a different world and have to be taken off like a coat, when we go outside into the 'real world'. Then we come back in and put them on again.

In *The Economist* magazine in Easter week 1999 there was an article about Jesus in an "Obituary" column. The article, which was not overtly hostile, mentioned that Christianity was by far the world's largest religion, claiming 1.9 billion adherents. The last paragraph of the article said:

> Nearly two billion people unblushingly call themselves Christian, happily breaking almost every commandment should the occasion arise, serving Mammon and goodness knows who else. (*The Economist*)

Is that the way it is among Christians? That should not be, as we see from 1 Timothy 6:11.

> But you, *Man of God*, flee from all this, and pursue righteousness, godliness, faith, love, endurance and gentleness.

As Christians, Timothy and we should seek to establish our value systems on the same basis as the Lord, turning our backs on the god of consumerism and placing priority on what He regards as important, such as the six virtues identified by Paul in this verse. Paul's approach here is striking. He addresses Timothy as "*Man of God*", and the emphasis in the sentence is on the word "you"; you, Timothy, the *Man of God*, in contrast to the man of the world. The qualities listed are also striking.

- Righteousness: That is moral uprightness.
- Godliness: Genuine Christ-likeness
- Faith, love and endurance: These 3 occur together in Titus 2:2, where they are included as part of the qualities that Titus was to teach to "old men". They also occur together in 1 Thessalonians 1:3, as the supreme characteristics of the Thessalonian Christians.
- Gentleness: An attitude of calm reasonableness, especially in the face of hostile argument, which is designed to lead someone to repentance. (See 2 Timothy 2:25).

When we take these six characteristics of the true believer together, we find that they cover every aspect of the balanced Christian life.

- The aspects of our character: moral uprightness and a genuine Christ-likeness lived out on a daily basis.
- The inner strengths of faith and endurance, which underpin consistent godliness.
- The attitude of gentleness towards those we encounter, which stems from the work of grace in our own lives.

So these are the attitudes Timothy is to develop in contrast to the outlook of these false teachers. But Paul's concern for Timothy is not just that he should turn away from having a wrong view about money.

3. Flee the evil desires of youth

In 2 Timothy 2:22, as in the previous passage, the warning is immediately followed by the positive alternative.

> Flee the evil desires of youth, and pursue righteousness, faith, love and peace, along with those who call on the Lord out of a pure heart.

Timothy was relatively young and had been thrust into a very important situation. In 1 Timothy 4:12, Paul warns him not to let anyone look down on him because he is young. So Timothy might lack the experience and maturity to cope with some situations and could easily come to grief.

The obvious danger to undisciplined youth is sexual temptation, but this does not seem to be uppermost in Paul's mind, because of the positive virtues that he chooses to set in contrast to the "evil desires". The risks that Paul would appear to be thinking of are most likely to be the intolerance and impatience of youth, its love of novelties and of argument. Instead of such an outlook, Timothy is given a further four positive qualities to develop together with a pure heart—righteousness, faith, love and peace. The first three have already come up together in 1 Timothy 6:11, in connection with the dangers of a love of money.

Paul adds a fourth quality to these, the seeking for peace. This would be particularly important in an environment where there was so much arguing and quarrelling. The *Man of God* must not participate in this, but should at all times seek to live at peace, especially with those who call upon God from a pure heart.

The approach set out here, as Towner (p187) says, is genuine godliness. The word "godliness" itself is not used in the passage, but it effectively sums up what is being described; i.e. moral uprightness, with our thinking processes and our moral decision-making pure and untainted by the half truths and double think of self-centredness. It is a living relationship with God, in and through Christ, on the vertical axis (righteousness and faith), and an outworking of that relationship with our fellow men on the horizontal axis (love and peace).

The first three dangers that we have considered are all barriers to the growth of true godliness in the life of the *man* or *woman of God* because they divert us away from the thought patterns and priorities that are critical to the pursuit of godliness. Rather than follow the futile self-discipline involved in the pursuit of myth, Timothy must train himself for godliness. Rather than seeking to develop his earthly wealth, Timothy must work for the "great gain" that comes from godliness with contentment. Rather than allowing the desires and passions of youth to be the dominant features of his thinking and conduct, Timothy must pursue the development of godliness; i.e. righteousness and faith in his relationship with God, and love and peace in his relationship with men and women.

In the church at Ephesus, as in many Christian groups today, there was a love of discussion and argument. While there is much to be gained from a discussion on the things of God, there are dangers attaching to certain types of debate. Two of these Timothy was asked to avoid:

4. Avoid foolish and stupid arguments

> Don't have anything to do with foolish and stupid arguments, because you know they produce quarrels. (2 Timothy 2:23)

This is not the only place where we see this warning about quarrels. We have already considered 1 Timothy 6:3, where Paul writes about individuals who teach false doctrine, with particular emphasis on a wrong emphasis on wealth.

> If anyone teaches false doctrines and does not agree to the sound instruction of our Lord Jesus Christ and to godly teaching, he is conceited and understands nothing. He has an unhealthy interest in controversies and quarrels about words that result in envy, strife, malicious talk, evils suspicions and constant friction between men of corrupt mind, who have been robbed of the truth. (1 Timothy 6:3-5)

What is involved in "false doctrine" is not exactly clear, but it appears that the people Paul has in mind took it upon themselves to have a private theology that flies in the face of all arguments. This he regards as total arrogance, and a definite indication that they have no real understanding. When one compared their doctrine to that of "sound instruction", it was infinitely inferior, and their conduct matched it.

This passage also gives us insight into the sort of arguments Paul regarded as "foolish and stupid". They consisted of undisciplined, possibly speculative wrangling about words and other peripheral theological issues for which no conclusive solution was available. And here in 1 Timothy

6:4-5 we can see the evil attitudes that result from such arguments, but that should not be the way of the Lord's servant. And when we turn back to 2 Timothy 2, once again the contrast is there. He has said in verse 23 that Timothy should avoid foolish speculations because they produce quarrels. Then we get the positive alternative in the next verse.

> And the Lord's servant must not quarrel; instead, he must be kind to everyone, able to teach, not resentful. Those who oppose him he must gently instruct, in the hope that God will grant them repentance leading them to a knowledge of the truth, and that they will come to their senses and escape from the trap of the devil, who has taken them captive to do his will. (2 Timothy 2:24-26)

The attitude of the Christian is to be consistent.

- Kind to everyone: Gentle, kindly.
- An understanding teacher (which 1 Timothy 3:2 gives as a characteristic of a bishop, *KJV*, or overseer, *NIV*).
- Not resentful: Forbearing: Patient under wrongs (Weymouth).

The context here is the situation where people involve themselves in debate and argument, about detailed trivia in theological issues. The *Man of God* is expected not to rail at them for their folly or their heresy. Instead, he should show a gentle spirit, not ruffled by the folly or the persuasiveness of the arguments, not reacting when the argument becomes personalised, as it surely will do in that situation, but calmly and patiently pointing out (in Timothy's case) the apostolic truth.

Now that advice is extremely appropriate to the present day, because in church Bible study groups, as well as in discussion with people in all walks of life, we will come across some bizarre theologies, often privately developed, often very emotionally argued, and often poorly thought out. These theories are sometimes based on an over-emphasis on a single verse taken out of context, if they have any scriptural backing at all. But our reaction must always be consistent; i.e. an unruffled gentle approach, pointing out error and maintaining our temper, and a positive attitude towards these people, even if they abuse us. And why should the *Man of God* have this attitude? Because, as verses 25 and 26 tell us, his primary aim is that these people should see the truth and repent. This is not something that will happen if they are bruised and beaten in an argument. Our Master is not willing that any should perish or that their lives should be wasted. We do not have the power to bring them to repentance by our arguments, but it is our job, as *men and women of God*, to put nothing in the way, which would prevent the Lord from working.

Earlier in chapter 2, Paul also warns Timothy about the problems of quarrelling about words.

> Warn them before God against quarrelling about words; it is of no value, and only ruins those who listen. (2 Timothy 2:14)

Here two reasons are given as to why people should not quarrel about words.

- It is of no value: because of the corrupt motives, ludicrous arguments and trivial subject matter. It adds nothing and no good comes from it.
- It "undermines the faith" (Phillips) of those who hear them.

In the earlier passages we considered, Paul said that arguments are to be avoided because of the atmosphere they generate. Timothy is to avoid getting involved in them, and instead has to bring people to a point of repentance. But in 2 Timothy 2:14 there is another note, avoiding arguments because of the damage they do to people's faith. In 1 Timothy 6, he spoke about the malice, suspicions and constant friction that arguments cause. That can destroy people's faith, by disillusioning them. Also, some can be persuaded by the fine-sounding arguments and if these arguments appeal to their intellect, or some other part of their nature, they may be tempted to turn away from the truth of the gospel. There are some arguments I have heard that I would like to be true, either because they appeal to me, or they would solve a lot of problems, or they would make life a lot easier. There is a risk that Christians who are not grounded in the truth will lap up such notions. This idea of corrupt doctrines corrupting people is picked up again in the same chapter.

5. Avoid godless chatter

> Avoid godless chatter, because those who indulge in it will

become more and more ungodly. Their teaching will spread like gangrene. Among them are Hymenaeus and Philetus, who have wandered away from the truth. They say that the resurrection has already taken place, and they destroy the faith of some. (2 Timothy 2:16-18)

Here the emphasis is not so much on damaged relationships and attitudes, but on people becoming "ungodly", and it relates to what people believe. The imagery is very striking: the progression of increasing ungodliness and the comparison to gangrene, spreading throughout the whole body. An example is given of this sort of teaching, that of Hymenaeus and Philetus (verses 17-18). What exactly this heresy was, or how it could destroy people's faith, is not clear. In 2 Thessalonians 2:2-3, Paul mentions another false idea that was causing problems, that the day of the Lord had already come. It's possible that these two heresies were linked, but it is difficult to be certain. Hymenaeus also appears in 1 Timothy 1:20, where we read that Paul "handed him over to Satan, that he may learn not to blaspheme". Obviously when 2 Timothy was written, he was still doing his work, and all this stems from "godless chatter", a phrase that comes up again in 1 Timothy 6:20-21.

Turn away from godless chatter and the opposing ideas of what is falsely called knowledge, which some have professed and in doing so have wandered from the faith.

The instruction here is very similar to 2 Timothy 2:16. Timothy is urged to avoid such conversations because they are connected with a spurious form of knowledge and lead to a wandering away from the faith.

This is Paul's final comment to Timothy at the end of his first letter. He has been warning him against this sort of problem throughout the letter, and when he comes to the end, he repeats the warning because of its importance. He says it at the end and, in fact, he says it right at the beginning of 1 Timothy.

Stay there in Ephesus so that you may command certain men not to teach false doctrines any longer nor to devote themselves to myths and endless genealogies. These promote controversies rather than God's work—which is by faith. The goal of this command is love, which comes from a pure heart and a good conscience and a sincere faith. Some have wandered away from these and turned to meaningless talk. They want to be teachers of the law, but they do not know what they are talking about or what they so confidently affirm. (1 Timothy 1:3-7)

The errors and their dangers are set out before us.

- False doctrines, myths and genealogies. Here we are back to some of the problems encountered in 1 Timothy 4: godless myths.
- As a result - controversy, rather than God's work
- Meaningless talk and ignorance.

So what is to be Timothy's positive reaction to this? Timothy was asked to oppose this error and to command these people to stop teaching it (verse 3). But the purpose of making this command is set out in verse 5. It is to create an environment where love can flourish among the congregation at Ephesus, in contrast to the dissensions and arguing about words. This love comes from three sources and the Greek emphasises "out of" three things.

- A pure heart (specially singled out in the Sermon on the Mount as being a characteristic of those who will see God). In Scripture, the heart stands for the totality of man's entire mental and moral activity. If purity is lacking there, he cannot be a source of Christian love (Kelly p46).
- A good conscience (the ability to judge oneself, in contrast to those in 1 Timothy 4:2, whose consciences were seared with a hot iron).
- A genuine faith (also mentioned in 2 Timothy 1:5, as being a characteristic Timothy possessed, as did his grandmother and mother).

The heretical teaching of these men was not only causing error in belief, which was bad enough, but was causing unrest within the Christian community. Therefore Timothy had to act firmly to stamp it out.

An overview

If we, like Timothy, are to be *men and women of God*, we must avoid the ways of the world, which show themselves in the religion of the natural man, with its emphasis on discipline of the body, punishing it and depriving it of certain things. Paul explains that this false religiosity also shows itself in following the teaching of deceiving spirits, and in stupid arguments about unimportant issues. These cause double damage because first of all they lead people away from the truth and into meaningless talk and ignorance. Secondly, they also cause quarrelling and a worldly attitude that has to be avoided. Timothy is to flee the evil desires of youth, with its intolerance and its love of argument. He is also to avoid the desire of the man of the world for wealth, supposing that religion is a means of financial gain. In contrast to these, godliness with contentment is great gain. It probably will not be financial gain, but in the final analysis, the pursuit of godliness is the recipe for a life that is not only rewarding, but has real value into eternity. Therefore Timothy, the *Man of God*, is asked to follow after that.

The pursuit of godliness, with its vertical dimension of faith towards God and its horizontal dimension of attitudes of gentleness, non-retaliation, constant seeking of the good of those who abuse us, is set before Timothy and us as something to be "trained" for. Contentment is something Paul "learned". These things are not easy, but we have to learn to flee from the things that can damage us, and focus our minds on what is helpful in building us up.

Above all is the issue of doctrine. This is particularly important to Timothy, who is in charge of the church at Ephesus. He is to keep away from the doctrines of demons, and he is to command and teach the true apostolic message, and also to command those who would do so not to teach error. But in 2 Timothy 4, Paul looks forward to the point when such false doctrine will reach its climax.

> For the time will come when men will not put up with sound doctrine. Instead, to suit their own desires, they will gather around them a great number of teachers to say what their itching ears want to hear. They will turn their ears away from the truth and turn aside to myths. (2 Timothy 4:3-4)

By the time 2 Timothy was written, Paul was experiencing rejection on all sides. All in Asia had deserted him and his message (1:15), and many of his trusted friends had left him (4:10). He expected execution very soon (4:6). Against this background he could speak with bitter experience of a threefold decline.

- An intolerance of sound doctrine
- An emphasis on teaching that appealed to the listeners
- A preoccupation with myth at the expense of truth

Whether Paul was speaking of his own time, or prophetically about the future, we cannot be sure. However, we are today in a situation where the tide of opposition to Christian truth is rising ever higher, and the issues Paul highlights are all relevant. That is not to say that Paul necessarily had our present age in mind when he wrote. Opposition to the Word and authority of God, in whatever form it takes, evidences these characteristics once it reaches its worst point.

In our post-modern age there is a refusal to accept authority in moral teaching. 'Organised religion' is under deep suspicion and is perceived as constituting a restriction on personal freedom. Christian doctrines expressed as revealed, authoritative truth are abhorrent to this way of thinking. Also, the relativism that accompanies this approach to truth means that people look to be given concepts and values that they can accept or reject as they choose, without penalty. People wish to be affirmed in their lifestyles, rather than challenged. Thirdly, post-modernism is concerned with the deconstruction of historic events, objects and religious statements, and gives them a subjective meaning that is helpful to one individual, but which may validly be given a different 'spin' by someone else. Truth, as the Scriptures would understand it, is turned into myth.

People with such an outlook do become involved with the Christian faith, for certain aspects of it appeal. However, they bring with them the 'deconstruction' process and apply it to the Scriptures. Verses are taken out of context and are given a meaning that is totally alien to the passage. Faced with a situation like that, how do we approach these people with the truth in Christ? Paul here envisages a total departure from sound truth, and he sets out his instructions to Timothy in 2 Timothy 4:5.

> But you, keep your head in all situations, endure hardship, do the
> work of an evangelist, discharge all the duties of your ministry.

The contrast is clearly stated. The emphasis in the Greek text, as in the English, is on the opening words in the sentence. "You, Timothy, in contrast..." And as in the danger in arguing about words, so with false doctrine, Timothy had to remain alert and in control of himself when dealing with these people. And the alertness needed is at least partly to do with the risk of being carried away by the new-fangled ideas.

Paul's answer to false doctrine is, of course, true doctrine, which will be considered in the next chapter. But care must be taken on how this is put across. Timothy was not under obligation to convert people (and neither are we). He was asked to set out the truth in a reasonable, kind and gracious manner, and then to step back and let God's Spirit work. Timothy's whole approach was to avoid exacerbating a situation where there was more heat than light. His ultimate aim was the repentance of his opponents, and he had a duty to do nothing that would make this less likely, and I would suggest that our responsibility is the same.

We always have to remember when we are in situations that we are not just dealing with a philosophical theory. We are dealing with a living Word, and a living God Who has promised that His Word will not return to Him empty, but will achieve His purposes. We, therefore, have a duty to set out the truth in a manner that is intelligible to our listeners, and leave the consequences to Him. Timothy was thus to avoid the dangers of wrong teaching, unhelpful arguments and inappropriate desires, but he was also to avoid certain people:

6. Have nothing to do with these people

> There will be terrible times in the last days. People will be lovers of themselves, lovers of money, boastful, proud, abusive, disobedient to parents, ungrateful, unholy, without love, unforgiving, slanderous, without self-control, brutal, not lovers of the good, treacherous, rash, conceited, lovers of pleasure rather than lovers of God—having a form of godliness but denying its power. Have nothing to do with them. (2 Timothy 3:1-5)

Paul speaks here of the "last days", and these verses are usually interpreted as a prediction of conditions immediately prior to Christ's return. This phrase is used of the end times in Acts 2:17, James 5:3 and 2 Peter 3:3. Also, in John 6:39,40 and 44, the phrase "last day" is used of the day of resurrection. Alternatively, Paul could have meant nothing more technical than "ultimately", or "finally", as the Greek *eschatos* (last), can be used in the sense of the last in a series (as in 1 Corinthians 15:8). Certainly Paul expects Timothy to experience these conditions (verse 5).

Whether or not Paul thought he was living in the last days, the list of evil characteristics is formidable. And it's important to realise how easily Timothy could be deceived by people like this if he was unprepared. Verse 5 indicates that they have a "form of godliness", but without the power. Verse 6 shows that they are skilled manipulators.

> They are the kind who worm their way into homes and gain control over weak-willed women, who are loaded down with sins and are swayed by all kinds of evil desires, always learning but never able to acknowledge the truth. (2 Timothy 3:6-7)

It is difficult to know what the context of this is. But it would appear that these false teachers sought out women of a particular type, who were "loaded down with sins" (in the sense of being "overwhelmed in their conscience", Guthrie p158) rather than particularly evil. They were thus prepared to clutch at any straws offered, but their thinking had become so distorted that they were incapable of discerning truth from falsehood and therefore were easy prey to any high sounding nonsense that came along. They were therefore unable to come to any knowledge of the truth.

Numerous attempts have been made to draw parallels between incidents and trends in our society today and the vices listed in this passage. The truth is that down through the ages there have been many men of depraved minds (from the time of Jannes and Jambres) who have opposed the truth (verse 8) and have led many astray. So how was Timothy to know what was truth and what was falsehood?

> You, however, know all about my teaching, my way of life, my purpose, faith, patience, love, endurance, persecutions, sufferings ... as for you, continue in what you have learned and have become convinced of, because you know those from whom you learned it, and how from infancy you have known the holy Scriptures, which are able to make you wise for salvation through faith in Christ Jesus. (2 Timothy 3:10-11,14-15)

The contrast is strong, and obvious. Timothy has been instructed by Paul and others, and in these verses Paul tells him to continue in what he has learned. Timothy has two strong grounds for remaining convinced of the truth of what he has been taught.

- The trustworthiness of those from whom he learned it, and
- the consistency of the teaching with the Scriptures he had been taught from infancy.

These two grounds give Timothy (and us) an antidote to all the false teaching and deception we could meet.

Questions for discussion and meditation

1. What is the role of the conscience in the development of godliness in the life of the Christian? (p6). How are faith and conscience linked?

2. In what areas of life do you feel the tension between the claims of Christ and the materialism of the world? What principles can we establish to help us to make the right decisions? (pp7-10)

3. Think about the need for a consistency between our relationship with God and our relationship with one another (p10). What are the danger points at which inconsistencies creep in?

4. How would you distinguish valid theological discussion from "foolish and stupid arguments" and "godless chatter" (pp12-16).

5. Think about the ways in which the present day approaches to "truth" affect people's reaction to the message of the Gospel (p17-18).

Doctrine and Conduct: The Influence of Others

At the close of the last chapter we considered the twofold means by which Timothy could be sure of the truth of his doctrine as set out in 2 Timothy 3. This is part of a longer section dealing with the comprehensive equipping of the *Man of God* for service, and the whole section is quoted here for ease of reference:

> Evil men and impostors will go from bad to worse, deceiving and being deceived. But as for you, continue in what you have learned and have become convinced of, because you know those from whom you learned it, and how from infancy you have known the holy Scriptures, which are able to make you wise for salvation through faith in Christ Jesus. All Scripture is God-breathed and is useful for teaching, rebuking, correcting and training in righteousness, so that the *Man of God* may be thoroughly equipped for every good work. (2 Timothy 3:13-17)

Timothy's doctrine came to him from two sources.

- From people on whom he could depend, and
- from Scripture.

Scripture, correctly applied, is the sole arbiter in determining doctrine. However, I would suggest that most of us owe our understanding of Christian truth, not only to sitting in our studies alone with the Word, but to listening to and discussing matters with other Christians whose judgment and understanding we respect. So it was with Timothy. Timothy was told that there were certain types of people he should have nothing to do with, because they would damage his ability to be an effective *Man of God*. But here Paul tells him that one of the bases for knowing that what he believes is true is the quality of those who taught him. In this chapter we will consider the influence of other *men and women of God* on Timothy's understanding, and in the next chapter we will look at the influence of Scripture. Who were the people who had taught Timothy, and how was this process expected to continue? First of all, there was his family. 2 Timothy 2:15 tells us that "from infancy" he had been brought up in the truth.

The influence of Timothy's family

We learn more of this from 2 Timothy 1:5.

> I have been reminded of your sincere faith, which first lived in
> your grandmother Lois and in your mother Eunice and, I am
> persuaded, now lives in you also.

Timothy's mother and grandmother were obviously major influences on
Timothy's life of faith. More of the family background is given us in Acts
16.

> He (Paul) came to Derbe and then to Lystra, where a disciple
> named Timothy lived, whose mother was a Jewess and a believer,
> but whose father was a Greek. The brothers at Lystra and Iconium
> spoke well of him. Paul wanted to take him along on the journey,
> so he circumcised him because of the Jews who lived in that area,
> for they all knew that his father was a Greek. (Acts 16:1-3)

Timothy's mother was Jewish, and had converted to Christianity although
his father was a Greek (and by implication, not a believer), but by marrying
a pagan and not circumcising her son, she had effectively put herself
outside the Jewish community. At what stage she became a Christian is not
clear, but some commentators suggest that Acts 16:1 indicates that she was
a widow and the implication was that she became a Christian some time
after her husband's death. It was therefore presumably through his mother
that the Jewish scriptures and the truth of the Christian Gospel had been
given to Timothy. That was his inheritance of faith through his family.

The influence of Paul

If Timothy's father was dead, then perhaps Paul's description of Timothy
as his "son" becomes even more poignant. Paul was like a father to
Timothy, and much of what Timothy learned was from Paul, both in terms
of doctrine and lifestyle. For example, in 2 Timothy 1 we read:

> What you heard from me, keep as the pattern of sound teaching,
> with faith and love in Christ Jesus. Guard the good deposit that

was entrusted to you—guard it with the help of the Holy Spirit who lives in us. (2 Timothy 1:13-14)

The pattern of sound teaching and the good deposit

The Greek word for "pattern" means an outline or a basic sketch by an artist, or a first draft by a writer. It could also be like a blueprint by an architect (Hanson p80). It is an outline rather than a detailed creed to be recited word for word, and, although he has to stick to the principles that Paul lays out, and use it as a framework, Timothy is free to expound it in his own words. Paul's own teaching is to be no more than a starting point (Guthrie p132). The message of Christ has to be expressed in a way that communicates to the culture within which we live, or it will be perceived as being irrelevant by the people living in that culture. This principle has the backing of Scripture: Paul's address on Mars Hill is very different from his message to a Jewish audience, for example. However, we have to take care that the message itself is not compromised. That is why Timothy (and we) have to keep a firm hold of the basic pattern so that we can make the teaching relevant to where people are without distorting the message.

But there is another phrase that occurs in verse 13. It is "with faith and love". To what does this refer? The most natural reading in English is that he is to "keep" it with faith and love, and if so, it shows the manner in which Timothy is expected to hold on to his doctrine. He cannot be lax about it, but the way he relates to others must be characterised by faith and love. The two go together. Paul has already mentioned them in 1 Timothy 1:14 and we also see them together in 1 Thessalonians 1:3.

But on the other hand, this "pattern" Timothy received from Paul is a pattern of "sound *teaching*", which suggests the communication of this message, rather than simply the holding on to it. So Paul could mean that the *teaching* of this message should be with faith and love. And Timothy's responsibility is to do these two things—keep it, and teach it.

In 2 Timothy 1:13, Timothy is asked to "keep" this pattern. And the meaning is really "hold fast", and Paul goes on in verse 14 to tell him to "guard" the good deposit—keep it safe from distortion or corruption by the false teachers of whom Paul warns Timothy. It seems reasonable to equate the "good deposit" with the "pattern of sound teaching". But where did this "deposit" come from? In 2 Timothy 1:11-12 we read:

Of this gospel I was appointed a herald and an apostle and a teacher. That is why I am suffering as I am. Yet I am not ashamed, because I know whom I have believed, and am convinced that he is able to guard what I have entrusted to him for that day.

Verse 12 is very well-known. It is usually interpreted as meaning that God is able to keep Paul's "soul" safe until the Day of Judgment, that Paul is eternally secure. Now, our eternal future in Christ *is* secure, and that is something to rejoice in, but it may not be what Paul is saying here.

Because "what I have committed to him" could equally be translated "what he has committed to me", and is in fact "my deposit" (the same word as in verse 14). In other words it could refer to the special revelation and pattern of sound words which had been entrusted to Paul. And since that is the context of verse 11 and verse 13, it would seem more likely. It would appear somewhat out of place for Paul, in the middle of seriously urging Timothy to hold fast to sound doctrine, to suddenly become preoccupied with his own personal security.

God had given Paul a "deposit" of truth, and Paul is confident that God is able to preserve that deposit from being corrupted (verse 12). Paul, in his turn, has passed it on to Timothy, and he urges Timothy to keep it safe within himself, and guard it with the help of the Holy Spirit who lives in him (verse 14). But Timothy has another responsibility in relation to this deposit.

> And the things you have heard me say in the presence of many witnesses entrust to reliable men who will also be qualified to teach others. (2 Timothy 2:2)

Timothy has a duty not only to guard the deposit, but also to pass it on, and the word translated "entrust" in verse 2 is the verbal form of "deposit". The progression can be traced. Paul, with the help of the Lord, is guarding the deposit in himself and passing it on to Timothy. Timothy in his turn is to guard it with the Lord's help, and also deposit it on others. But he is to be careful to whom he passes on the deposit. It is to "reliable" men, who will, in their turn, be able to deposit it on others. The "deposit" is the message entrusted to Paul who was the apostle of the Gentiles. Welch says:

> This entrusted truth is associated with Paul as the Prisoner of Jesus Christ with a purpose that goes back before age times, and

with himself as the accredited Preacher, Apostle and Teacher of the Gentiles. These features link the good deposit with the truth revealed in Ephesians, where Paul is again spoken of as the Prisoner of Christ Jesus, where the purpose goes back to before the foundation of the world, and where the truth entrusted is described as "The Mystery" (Ephesians 3:1-14) for which he also suffered (Welch p70).

Timothy was in Ephesus, a largely Gentile city, and therefore the pattern, the deposit of truth for the Gentiles, was particularly relevant. Timothy, here in verse 14, is to guard it with the help of the Spirit, who lives in us.

At the time Paul was writing the New Testament had not been formalised. The writings of the apostles were certainly recognised as Scripture. For example, in 2 Peter 3:16, Peter refers to Paul's writings as "Scripture". Where information was received by revelation, as in Paul's case, it was important that this was passed on intact and without corruption, and this required not only diligent effort on the part of Paul, Timothy and his successors, but also the help of the Spirit to preserve the truth. The Lord was not prepared to allow His message to be corrupted.

But there was a further danger because many other letters, histories and treatises were being written, and these were not inspired like the writings of Paul and the other apostles. In fact, some of them were extremely suspect. Throughout the writings of the early church, warnings against corruption of doctrine are evident, and they were very real warnings. Paul, John, Peter and Jude all warn against the dangers of false teaching. The material in the epistles to Timothy gives us an idea of the extent of Paul's concern about this issue.

So against the background of revelation of new truth and a great deal of corruption and false ideas, one of the foundations on which Timothy could base his trust in the truth of what he heard was the quality of the people from whom he heard it. And Timothy was here being encouraged to maintain that tradition of seeking out reliable people who could be entrusted with this message.

In addition, the way in which Timothy is to "guard" the truth and to teach it is to be one of faith and love which comes from being in Christ Jesus. There is to be no rigid judgmentalism, but Timothy's attitude to all opposition, even of the most obstinate and abusive kind, is to be gentle, persuasive, kind and caring. This is the attitude that Timothy has to have both in guarding the deposit, and in passing it on. This is the attitude of Christ, and it is also the hallmark of the *Man of God*.

Trustworthy sayings

But how is the message preserved and passed on like this? There are particular ways in which Paul helps Timothy to remember the key issues of the faith. One of these is the use of little proverbs that Paul describes as "trustworthy sayings".

> This particular formula is unusual and occurs nowhere else in Scripture apart from the epistles to Timothy and Titus. There are 4 different "trustworthy sayings" in 1 and 2 Timothy and 1 in Titus (3:8). What Paul seems to be doing is quoting "in a rhythmical form, a statement current in the churches" (Guthrie p65), possibly a statement of doctrine which was used for teaching purposes, or a hymn (Hanson p27).

In view of Paul's emphasis (e.g. in Galatians 1:11-12) on the fact that his gospel was given to him by revelation, it is unlikely that he was appealing to someone else's work to give authentication to his own views. He was most likely reminding Timothy of a sort of early catechism that was well known to him. Important truth was summarised in a brief verse, which was perhaps more easily remembered than the involved arguments in Paul's writings. So these "trustworthy sayings" would obviously contain really important truths, well expressed and honed down to cover the essential elements. The first of these is found in 1 Timothy 1:15.

Christ Jesus came into the world to save sinners

> Here is a trustworthy saying that deserves full acceptance: Christ Jesus came into the world to save sinners—of whom I am the worst.

Here the trustworthy saying is given a further attribute, that it deserves full acceptance, an expression which is also added to one of the other sayings (1 Timothy 4:9).

As one might expect, the content of the "saying" is the very essence of the Gospel, but it shows us a very important truth that we do well to remember. Paul was always emphasising the fact that his gospel came by special revelation. He did not receive it from man but from God. But although this was a special revelation, his gospel is rooted in the historical, earthly work of the Lord Jesus Christ.

There is a risk that if we spend most of our time thinking about the truths revealed to Paul and the other apostles, we can lose sight of the basic fact that, without the incarnation, the earthly ministry, death and resurrection of the Lord in space and time, we have nothing but another vague philosophy. The Christian message, preached by the apostle to the Gentiles, is based on the historical events of the coming of the Lord Jesus to His own people Israel, and His rejection by that people.

Of course, this is not the *only* place in Paul's writings where he mentions the Lord's first advent (see, for example 2 Timothy 1:10), but it is not common in his epistles. However, it is noteworthy that this appears right at the start of his first letter to Timothy. So the very essence of Paul's gospel to the Gentiles is that Christ came to save sinners, and he adds here that he is "the worst", and that he owes his position—as we all do—to the mercy of God.

In 1 Timothy 3:1, we have a second "trustworthy saying".

The work of a bishop is a noble task

The word "bishop" is a far cry from our current usage of that word. It is a fairly general one and probably refers to anyone who had a position of responsibility in the church. Churches therefore had a number of bishops, rather than one controlling bishop (Allen p277). For example the Philippian church had bishops and deacons (Philippians 1:1). Paul appears to quote this well-known saying for two main reasons:

- to emphasise the importance of the position of church leaders, and
- to reinforce the need for church leaders to be high quality individuals, with the qualities that he is going to describe in the next few verses.

And the qualities are expressed not in terms of the skills they possessed, but in terms of the aspects of their character.

The overseer must be above reproach, the husband of but one wife, temperate, self-controlled, respectable, hospitable, able to teach, not given to drunkenness, not violent but gentle, not quarrelsome, not a lover of money. He must manage his own family well and see that his children obey him with proper respect....He must not be a recent convert, or he may become conceited and fall under the same judgment as the devil. He must also have a good reputation with outsiders, so that he will not fall into disgrace and into the devil's trap. (1 Timothy 3:2-7)

These characteristics cover a wide variety of aspects of the overseer's life.

- The type of people they are: controlled, respectable, hospitable, gentle.
- Their home situation: one wife, obedient children.
- Their level of maturity: not a recent convert.
- Their standing in the non-Christian community: having a good reputation.

Timothy had been placed in a responsible position for the church in Ephesus. He was young and it was necessary that he put church leaders in place who were of the appropriate type. We have already noted Paul's instructions to Timothy on how he should treat the "deposit of truth", passing it on to *reliable* men who had the capacity to teach others. So here, the work of bishop (and, in verses 8-13, deacons also) was only to be given to men of the highest quality. In these verses we can see a glimpse of how this *reliability* works itself out in the different aspects of life.

Training for godliness represents the highest value

The third trustworthy saying is in 1 Timothy 4:8-10.

For physical training is of some value, but godliness has value for all things, holding promise for both the present life and the life to come. This is a trustworthy saying that deserves full acceptance (and for this we labour and strive) that we have put our hope in the living God, who is the Saviour of all men, and especially of those who believe.

There is some doubt as to what the "trustworthy saying" is. Some say that it is verse 10 (that we put our hope in the living God) and some that it is verse 8 (that we prize godliness above physical training). Verse 8 has more of an epigrammatical quality about it and, also, "for this we labour and strive" in verse 10 would appear to be more appropriate to training to be godly (verse 7) than to placing our hope in God.

So what are the issues here? The first "saying" relates to the gospel, and the nature of it. The second relates to the appointment of overseers to tend God's flocks. The third deals with the need for spiritual training to combat the false doctrines that were so prevalent. A lot of the false teaching related to these "godless myths" considered earlier, and involved teaching of rigorous abstinence, for example from certain foods and from marriage. The view was that the body could be controlled by a rigorous system of self-denial.

However, as Paul says here, while physical training has some value, it is surpassed by the benefits of "training in godliness". Godliness was earlier defined as genuine Christlikeness lived out on a daily basis. So the training in godliness is working at increased conformity to the nature of Jesus Christ, in a genuine way, where our lifestyle echoes our beliefs in a consistent manner, with no contradictions between them. That has infinitely superior value because, as Paul says in verse 8, it contains benefit both for this life, in giving purpose and fulfilment as well as health, and also for the life to come. The pursuit of godliness has value for eternity.

There is a fourth and final "trustworthy saying" in the epistles to Timothy, and that is in 2 Timothy 2:11-13.

The rewards of endurance and the shame of failure

Here is a trustworthy saying: If we died with him, we will also live with him; if we endure, we will also reign with him. If we disown him, he will also disown us; if we are faithless, he will remain faithful, for he cannot disown himself.

This is probably the best-known and best-loved of these sayings. There is a poetic rhythm here, though it does break up towards the end of verse 13, and it has been suggested that the poem itself ends in verse 12 and Paul adds his own concluding comments in verse 13.

The context here is the need to endure. The previous "saying" related to training for godliness and in verses 11-12 there are three ideas concerning the putting of that training into practice.

1. Dying leads to living: verse 11. It is unlikely that Paul was encouraging Timothy to be martyred. The idea is more along the lines of what he said in Romans 6 - the identification of the believer in the death and resurrection of Christ (see Romans 6:5). In fact there is a close parallel between Romans 6:8 and 2 Timothy 2:11

> Now if we died with Christ, we believe that we will also live with him. (Romans 6:8)

> If we died with him, we will also live with him (2 Timothy 2:11)

Christians are deemed to have died when Christ died and to have been raised to newness of life when Christ was raised. This has implications for our conduct here on earth. In Romans 6:12ff Paul develops this. Here too, in 2 Timothy 2:12, he moves on to the idea of suffering:

2. Suffering leads to reigning: verse 12. The type of suffering here is one of patient endurance. The emphasis is not so much on the suffering itself, but on our attitude towards it, and the kind of character it develops in us.

3. Denying leads to being denied: verse 12. This is an extremely sobering aspect of the Lord's relationship with His people. If we fail to take our place in suffering for Him and deny Him in our conduct He too will be ashamed of us when we stand before Him and we will suffer loss on that day.

In verse 13, a post-script is added: Our faithlessness does not affect His faithfulness. At this point the rhythm falters and it would appear that this verse is Paul's own addition to the poem. To follow the pattern Paul could have said that if our faith fails the Lord will not be faithful to us. But he cannot say that. It is not possible for the Lord to deny Himself or His promises to us. And that is where our ultimate security lies—not in our strength or ability to hold on, but in His faithfulness.

So there is a series of four "trustworthy sayings"—succinct comments written in a style that can be easily remembered. But the depth of meaning in these is tremendous. They are designed to help Timothy and others to stay on the road. In summary, the "trustworthy sayings" deal with:

- The content of the Gospel: rooted in Christ's earthly ministry and His work on the cross.
- The high honour and glory of those in positions of responsibility in the church, and therefore the characteristics that they should have.
- The need for dedication to training in godliness.
- The need for endurance and the rewards that await those who keep going.

But in addition we have the Lord's faithfulness underpinning our position and giving us security. If we are to be *men and women of God*, we must have a proper understanding of God's truth, so that we can distinguish the important from the unimportant, the good from the bad, or even more difficult, the best from the good.

We have both the Old and New Testament Scriptures, and, although Timothy was well-grounded in the Hebrew Scriptures and probably had some of Paul's letters (in addition to the ones written to himself), he was not in possession of the full canon. Therefore Timothy relied quite considerably on the message that was passed on to him verbally. Indeed, he himself was given the same instruction to pass it on, but to be careful to whom he delivered it.

And, although we have the completed Bible, it is still important for us to listen to others, those who, like Timothy, we have grown to respect on matters of doctrine and practice. These may be individuals who have the ability to produce a 'systematic theology', a way of showing us the 'Big Picture', or a framework for our faith, without which Christian doctrines appear random and confused. Others may have an extensive technical knowledge of Scripture (for example concerning the precise meanings of particular words). Others may by their insights be able to show us how to apply Christian truth in our daily conduct, so that we may know how best to "live a life worthy of the calling we have received" (Ephesians 4:1) in a post-modern age.

Similarly, songs, hymns and poems can express Christian truth in such a way as to give us a clearer vision, and can do so in a way that is memorable, and therefore very useful. Timothy was to use all of these. There are some hymns and songs today that are extremely powerful and express Christian truth brilliantly and memorably.

But on the other hand, although people can give insights into Scripture, if their conclusions cannot be demonstrated from Scripture, then they should be discarded. Their ideas may appeal to us, but they require to be tested against the touchstone of the Word of God. The same principle applies to songs: if their ideas correspond to Scripture they are very positive, but if not, we should not sing them, and there are a number of really popular Christian songs that are devoid of Scriptural content, and may even contradict the Word of God. Scripture is always the final arbiter, and Timothy was steeped in Scripture from infancy.

> ...from infancy you have known the holy Scriptures, which are able to make you wise for salvation through faith in Christ Jesus.
> (2 Timothy 3:15)

This is what gave him the ability to have confidence in the truth of what he believed, and the next section examines the place of Scripture in the life of the *Man of God*.

Questions for discussion and meditation

1. Spend some time considering people who have had a major influence on your understanding of Christian truth and give thanks to God for them. Who can you influence in similar ways and how best can you do it?

2. It is important that the "deposit" of truth given to Paul by the Lord and passed on by him to "faithful men" is not compromised by the changing fashions and philosophies of men. Yet at the same time, it is important that the message is presented in a manner that is relevant to the culture of the listeners (p24). In what ways is there a risk that the fundamental truths set out on pp25-26 (and others) may be distorted at the start of the twenty-first century? How do we guard against this?

3. What are the positive benefits of using poems, hymns and other sayings in rhythmic form for the communication of Christian truth (pp27-33)?

What are the risks?

4. Look at all aspects of the qualities Paul spells out for an overseer in 1 Timothy 3:2-7 (pp28-29). To what extent should these be applicable to all believers? How do we measure up?

Doctrine and Conduct: The Influence of Scripture

In 2 Timothy 3, Paul has a great deal to say about the nature and uses of Scripture.

> But as for you, continue in what you have learned and have become convinced of, because you know those from whom you learned it, and how from infancy you have known the holy Scriptures, which are able to make you wise for salvation through faith in Christ Jesus. All Scripture is God-breathed and is useful for teaching, rebuking, correcting and training in righteousness, so that the *Man of God* may be thoroughly equipped for every good work. (2 Timothy 3:14-17)

The first matter to be settled is what Paul means here by "Scripture"? The word he uses could mean any kind of writing, but it is used in the New Testament almost exclusively to mean the Old Testament Scriptures. These are what Timothy had drummed into him from infancy. However, it is noteworthy that the same word is also used to describe Paul's epistles in 2 Peter 3:16. So, the characteristics and uses of Scripture are equally applicable to the Old and New Testaments.

What is "inspiration"?

And the most striking characteristic of "Scripture" in 2 Timothy 3 is that it is "God-breathed", a word translated literally in the *New International Version*. The problem is to know what it means, since, although the word is used in secular Greek literature, it appears nowhere else in Scripture. The *King James Version* and many more modern English translations (e.g. *Moffatt, Weymouth, Phillips, New English Bible*) speak of Scripture being "inspired" or "given by inspiration", thereby avoiding an interpretation problem.

Kelly (p203) renders this phrase "literally meaning 'breathed into by God'", which carries with it the suggestion of something created separately being brought to life (as in Genesis 2:7). However, Macleod (p11) translates it as "breathed out by God", which perhaps more aptly captures the sense of God's input at the point of writing. The problem still remains to determine the role of the writer in the process. In classical Greek literature the 'inspired' writers were little more than writing tools in the hands of the gods. They acted merely as agents in transmitting the divinely given words to the page.

In 2 Peter 1:20-21, we are given some idea of how the process of 'inspiration' worked, in respect to prophecy at any rate.

> Above all, you must understand that no prophecy of Scripture came about by the prophet's own interpretation. For prophecy never had its origin in the will of man, but men spoke from God as they were carried along by the Holy Spirit.

There are interpretation problems with these verses, but verse 21 is paraphrased by Green as:

> No prophetic Scripture comes from self-inspired ecstasy, but from God.

If we interpret this as meaning "inspiration" in the Greek secular literature sense, one would expect everything to be written in the same style, since they are all by the same Author, with the writers being no more than writing instruments, transmitting directly dictated words. But that is clearly not the case. The work of Paul has certain characteristics (for example, the words and phrases used and his tendencies to use large parentheses). Similarly with the work of John, one can compare the fourth Gospel with John's epistles and see the common vocabulary and ideas. Throughout both Old and New Testaments the styles and personalities of the writers tend to come through. So the Scriptures bear something of the stamp of the writers in the work. They do not appear to be acting purely as the "mouthpiece" of God.

At the other extreme, one could suggest that it is only the ideas that are inspired. The individual words are not. Therefore there could be mistakes in Scripture and it would not matter. We may intuitively react against that idea by saying that since God is perfect, one would expect His inspired Word to be characterised by the same flawlessness. But the truth is that we are not explicitly told anywhere that that is what "inspiration" means. How can we decide?

The only way to decide is by looking at the way the Lord and the

Scripture writers speak of the Scriptures. First, in John 10:35, the Lord Jesus states that "the Scripture cannot be broken". He expands on this in Matthew 5:18:

> I tell you the truth, until heaven and earth disappear, not the smallest letter, not the least stroke of a pen, will by any means disappear from the Law until everything is accomplished.

This may be hyperbole, but what is the reality behind it? This is something much more than just the ideas. He is referring to the words themselves, even the individual letters. It becomes extremely dangerous for us to suggest that inspiration of Scripture means anything less stringent. We cannot read the New Testament without realising the high place that is given to Scripture. When Jesus started His ministry and was tempted by Satan in the wilderness, He answered each temptation with the statement "It is written..." (see, for example Matthew 4:4,7,10).

In John 17:17 Jesus, praying to His Father for His disciples says:

> Sanctify them by the truth; your word is truth.

Notice that He does not say God's Word is "true", which would be strong enough praise, but that it is "truth" itself.

These are only a few examples, but the point is that we would do well to give Scripture a similarly high position in our thinking, which means that we should consider all the words in the original manuscripts as being accurate, and treat the Greek and Hebrew manuscripts we have today with the highest regard. This does not mean, of course, that our English translations are perfect, and that is why we need to look carefully at a variety of reputable translations of the Greek and Hebrew Scriptures. We should also consider lexicons, dictionaries and other works of biblical scholars to see how problem verses and phrases are explained, and, having addressed the technical material, ask the Lord, through His Spirit, to reveal His truth to us. So the Scriptures, like no other book, are breathed out by God, and that is why people called them *The **Holy** Scriptures*. The full inspiration of Scripture is one of the tenets of The Open Bible Trust.

The usefulness of Scripture

Because the Scriptures are breathed out by God they are "useful" (verse 16b). The usefulness of the Scriptures in this passage is expressed in what they can accomplish for unbelievers in verse 15, and then in four purposes that they accomplish in connection with the sanctification of believers, in verse 16.

Usefulness for unbelievers (verse 15)

In 2 Timothy 3:15, Paul says that the Scriptures are able to make you wise for salvation through faith in Christ Jesus. It is important to realise that it is not the *Scriptures* that save us. Fundamental evangelicals have been accused of worshipping the Bible itself, but this is not the case. The Lord Jesus pointed out this error to the Jewish leaders.

> You diligently study the Scriptures because you think that by them you possess eternal life. These are the Scriptures that testify about me, yet you refuse to come to me to have life. (John 5:39-40)

The Scriptures tell us about the Lord and His purposes, and point to Christ. Scripture gives us the understanding that leads to faith towards Christ, and it is that which leads to salvation. This wisdom is in contrast to the "folly" that we read of in verse 9, in the minds of those who, as far as the faith is concerned, are rejected.

Usefulness for believers (verse 16)

Verse 16 indicates four ways in which Scripture builds up believers. Guthrie (p164) helpfully suggests that the first two relate to doctrine and the second two to conduct. Also, one of each pair is positive, and the other negative. The four ways can be set out in a table as follows:

	Positive	**Negative**
Doctrine	Teaching	Rebuking
Conduct	Training in righteousness	Correcting

The first function of Scripture in relation to the believer is that of teaching. The word means instructing people, primarily in doctrine. In 1 Timothy 4:13 we read:

> Until I come, devote yourself to the public reading of Scripture, to preaching and to teaching.

Teaching was one of Timothy's major remits, in his role as church leader in Ephesus, and we also must learn from Scripture in this respect. This is where our understanding of our faith comes from. The systematic teaching of Scripture is something that is lacking in a lot of our churches today, and it is perhaps not much consolation to see Paul warning Timothy in his second epistle that in the last days people will not put up with sound doctrine.

The second function is rebuking. This is the negative aspect of doctrine. If Scripture is the source of our doctrine, then a thorough knowledge of it will identify incorrect doctrine. Without an understanding of Christian truth as taught in Scripture, how can we be kept from accepting all sorts of wrong ideas? The Lord Jesus said to the Jews in Mark 12:24, "Are you not in error *because you do not know the Scriptures?*"

Christians without a comprehensive understanding of the Scriptures are open to believe error in a wide variety of forms. Many Christians do not have a systematic understanding of Christian truth. We learn a lot of particulars. But how do they fit together? Would we recognise an idea that was contrary to biblical teaching? Scripture gives us information by which we can test the truth of what we are told.

But Scripture also helps us in the way we live, in our conduct. The third and fourth functions of Scripture affect the believer's lifestyle. In the case of conduct, the negative aspect comes before the positive. The Scriptures offer correction to Christians in their behaviour. Repeatedly we are taught in Scripture that certain conduct is not appropriate for the Christian. This is either because it is unhelpful, or even damaging, to him or others, or because it is contrary to God's will, or because it is inappropriate to his standing in Christ. The Scriptures are the means by which our behaviour can be corrected.

The fourth and final work of Scripture in the life of the believer is to provide positive training in righteousness. We have seen the need for training in righteousness and the pursuit of righteousness as a feature of these epistles. In 1 Timothy 6:11, Paul says:

> But you, *Man of God*....pursue righteousness.

And again in 2 Timothy 2:22:

> Flee the evil desires of youth and pursue righteousness.

It is not easy to consistently behave as the Lord would want. We require training, and the Scriptures are the means of that training. The Scriptures give us constructive education in Christian life (Kelly p204). The word translated "training" suggests committed effort. In Hebrews 12 it occurs three times. It is translated "the *discipline* of the Lord" (verse 5). "Endure hardship as *discipline*" (verse 7). "No *discipline* seems pleasant, but painful" (verse 11).

The Scriptures are full of detailed instruction on how we should live. We are given systematic teaching on it; we are given good examples; we are given bad examples. But the aim of all our doctrine is ultimately that we will walk worthy of our calling. This is not just by believing the right things, but by living as Christ would have us to live. James expresses the need for us to persevere by constantly returning to the Word of God to be reminded of His truth.

> Do not merely listen to the word, and so deceive yourselves. Do what it says. Anyone who listens to the word but does not do what it says is like a man who looks at his face in a mirror and, after looking at himself, goes away and immediately forgets what he looks like. But the man who looks intently into the perfect law that gives freedom, and continues to do this, not forgetting what he has heard, but doing it—he will be blessed in what he does. (James 1:22-25)

Although the context of James's instructions is primarily the Law of Moses, the principle of constant returning to the Scripture for re-enforcement of the truth that we find there, is relevant to all ages. There are no easy routes to this blessing. It comes from a steady dedication to understanding and applying the teaching of Scripture to our lives on a daily basis.

The Word of God gives believers true doctrine and enables us to steer clear of error. It also serves to correct wrong conduct and to help in the training process towards greater Christ-likeness in our behaviour; in other words, to produce mature Christian manhood. Paul indicates this in verse 17 of 2 Timothy 3. The Scriptures are useful for these four purposes:

...so that the *Man of God* may be thoroughly equipped for every good work.

The Greek word that introduces this verse "so that" can denote either purpose or result. It is difficult to tell which, and it probably makes little practical difference, but the end result, whether by design or not, is that the *Man* or *Woman of God* is "thoroughly equipped" for every good work. This state of being equipped is variously translated "complete" (*RV*) or "perfect" (*KJV*) and is used for the complete equipment of a soldier going on active service. Obviously, the context has Timothy as the *Man of God*, in his role as the Christian leader, but there is no reason why what is said here should be limited to those with formal leadership responsibilities.

The Scriptures, which pointed Timothy to Christ, gave him the information to make sure that his doctrine was pure, and that his conduct matched it. If he continued on these two fronts, relying on the Scriptures to train him both in the understanding of God's truth and in the understanding of the way he should live, then he would be thoroughly prepared for this particular task, as we all should be. In 1 Timothy 4:15-16, we can see the two aspects of conduct and doctrine coming together.

Be diligent in these matters; give yourself wholly to them, so that everyone may see your progress. Watch your life and doctrine closely. Persevere in them, because if you do, you will save both yourself and your hearers.

"These matters" would appear to refer back to verse 13, namely the public reading of the Scriptures, teaching and preaching. By applying himself to the exposition of Scriptural doctrine and its application to his lifestyle in a diligent manner, Timothy would be working out his own salvation (as Paul expresses it in Philippians 2:12) and enabling others to do the same (Guthrie p99).

We have already noted the attitude Paul and the other New Testament writers had about Scripture, and here we see it in his instructions to Timothy. If the Scripture has such a high value—to give people the knowledge leading to salvation, and then to equip the believer in right conduct and doctrine, and to correct him when he goes wrong—one would expect Paul to advise Timothy to use Scripture a great deal in his ministry. And here in 1 Timothy 4:13, we have the public reading of Scripture. It is so important that people hear the Word and get used to it. There are three aspects of the public proclamation of the Word referred to in this verse: the reading of Scripture, exhortation and teaching. The first two were part of the Jewish heritage and were a feature of the synagogue service. The public reading of the Old Testament Scripture was usually followed by an exhortation. For example, in Luke 4:16, the Lord Jesus read the Scriptures and then commented on the passage. In Acts 13:15 there is a further example of this, where Paul, after the reading of the Scriptures, was invited to give a word of exhortation to the people.

But here in 1 Timothy 4, Paul adds "teaching". He anticipates that in Ephesus the reading of the Hebrew Scriptures would be followed by specific teaching of Christian doctrine, probably applying many of the Old Testament passages to Christ. And there was (and still is) a need for teaching like this, with all the false doctrines that were being taught within the Christian church there.

When Paul writes his second letter to Timothy we can see that this is still a major part of his instruction. In 2 Timothy 4:1-4 he writes:

> In the presence of God and of Christ Jesus, who will judge the living and the dead, and in view of his appearing and his kingdom, I give you this charge: Preach the Word; be prepared in season and out of season; correct, rebuke and encourage—with great patience and careful instruction. For the time will come when men will not put up with sound doctrine. Instead, to suit their own desires, they will gather around them a great number of teachers to say what their itching ears want to hear. They will turn their ears away from the truth and turn aside to myths.

Notice the solemnity with which Paul lays it on the line in verse 1. This reference to judgment is designed to concentrate Timothy's mind. There is an urgency for people to hear the true Gospel message because of the coming judgment, but also Timothy has to remember that he, and all other teachers will be judged on how they handle the Word, and the authenticity of their preaching and teaching.

Timothy has to persevere faithfully in season and out of season: i.e.

"whether the moment seems opportune or not" (Kelly p206) and there are three aspects to his work. He must correct (i.e. counter error in doctrine or conduct), rebuke (censure when necessary) and exhort (encourage his flock to continuation in the faith). And whatever approach he uses, it must be with patience and gentleness. He must always remain civil and unruffled in his dealings with people, and should develop the name of being a steady, faithful teacher of the Word, because, as Paul says in verses 3-4, life for the *Man of God* is going to get harder, until finally there will be a complete rejection of sound doctrine. Paul is in no doubt that the antidote to wrong ideas is the teaching of Scripture. That is the touchstone by which all our doctrine and our conduct can be assessed. If these are out of line with present day thinking—say on sexual morality—there is no doubt which we should follow.

The unashamed workman

In 2 Timothy 2:14 Paul has warned Timothy yet again about the dangers of meaningless arguing about words. Timothy is to remind people of the trustworthy saying in verses 11-13. Then in verse 15 Paul adds:

> Do your best to present yourself to God as one approved, a workman who does not need to be ashamed and who correctly handles the Word of Truth.

"Do your best" is probably a good rendering. The phrase recurs in 4:21.

> Do your best to get here before winter.

It is something that Timothy has to strive to accomplish. The *KJV*'s rendition "study" is misleading because it is not limited to studying of Scripture as some have tried to suggest. It is anything that has to be worked at. Studying of Scripture may be involved in it, but that is not the central point.

The passage says that he should do his best to present himself to God as one approved. There is a similarity here with the parable of the talents in Matthew 25. Here is the servant being called to present himself to his Master to account for his actions. He is to be presented before God as one who is tested and approved (the Greek word here can mean either). The contrast with the false teachers is very apparent. They sought the approval of men, whereas for the *Man of God,* it is only the Master's approval that counts for anything. The point at issue is the quality of his service.

So the verse continues by describing the servant as "a workman who does not need to be ashamed". The picture here is of a manual labourer, probably an agricultural worker, who has done his work well and can submit that work to his employer without any fear of an adverse reaction. This is something for all of us, no matter what our sphere of service is. Like the servants in the parable, like Timothy here, we will have to stand before the Lord to give account of our service. And we have to do our best to make sure that we will not be ashamed before Him on that day.

Rightly dividing

But what benchmark is there for Timothy to measure his own performance against, to see whether he will be an 'unashamed workman'? There is one important clue given at the end of verse 15. The unashamed workman is the one "who correctly handles the word of truth". The *NIV* translation is an interpretation. The *KJV*'s "rightly dividing" is nearer the original. But this is of little help as the meaning is not clear and the Greek word does not occur anywhere else in the New Testament. However it does occur twice in the *Septuagint*, the Greek translation of the Hebrew Scriptures. Both of these occurrences are in Proverbs:

> In all your ways acknowledge him, and he will *make your paths straight.* (Proverbs 3:6)

> The righteousness of the blameless *makes a straight way* for them. (Proverbs 11:5)

These passages suggest the idea of cutting out a straight road across uncharted territory. Applied to 2 Timothy 2:15 it would indicate the appropriate analysis of the Word of Truth; i.e. its accurate and straightforward interpretation and exposition and its appropriate application, in contrast to all the devious interpretations, distortions and abuses of the Word of Truth that were going on around.

The interpretation of this phrase as meaning the handling of the Word in a straightforward manner is picked up by a number of other translations. For example:

> ...a servant, who, because of his straightforward dealing with the word of truth, has no reason to feel any shame. (Weymouth)

> ...a workman who has kept to the straight line with the Message of Truth. (Schonfield)

> ...a labourer....who drives the ploughshare of truth in a straight furrow. (Way)

The particular subject that is at stake is the "Word of Truth". This phrase, like "rightly dividing", also occurs in two other places in Scripture - in Ephesians 1:13, and in the parallel passage in Colossians 1:5-6.

> ...in order that we, who were the first to hope in Christ, might be for the praise of his glory. And you also were included in Christ when you heard *the word of truth*, the gospel of your salvation. (Ephesians 1:12-13)

> ...the faith and love that spring from the hope that is stored up for you in heaven and that you have already heard about in *the word of truth*, the gospel that has come to you. All over the world this gospel is producing fruit and growing, just as it has been doing among you since the day you heard it and understood God's grace in all its truth. (Colossians 1:5-6)

So, in both these occurrences, the Word of Truth is the Gospel message that Timothy has to proclaim. So the criterion, by which the quality of Timothy's workmanship is to be judged, is the way in which he correctly analyses and presents the message as part of his work as an evangelist. But it is important to grasp the breadth of what is included in the Gospel message indicated in these passages in Ephesians and Colossians. The Gospel to these Gentile believers revealed to them "God's grace in all its truth", and told them of their heavenly hope, i.e. their calling as members of the Body of Christ.

The right division of the Word of Truth would, therefore, appear to indicate the straightforward presentation of the gospel in all its fullness, with no concessions to the fads and fashions of the day, with no corruption of the message delivered to Timothy by the apostle Paul.

Paul taught Timothy the importance of Scripture as the basis for his doctrine, because of the fact that it was God-breathed. It was able in the first instance to give him the wisdom leading to salvation through faith. It also had power for teaching Christian doctrine, for refuting error in belief; for pointing out the way he should behave and for rebuking people whose lifestyles were not as they should be. But this would only be possible if the Scriptural truth was properly applied. Otherwise, as many have found, the Bible can be used to teach anything.

Our responsibility, like that of Timothy, is to stick by the clear meaning of the Word in the face of opposition and cunningly developed arguments. It is not easy, and we have to learn rigour in our thinking, perseverance and dedication. This was a lesson for Timothy also, and, throughout the two epistles he, as a *Man of God*, was encouraged to carry on, to fight the good fight and keep on going, and this is the subject of the next chapter.

Questions for discussion and meditation

1. Why is it important that we have a proper understanding of "inspiration" of Scripture (pp35-37)?

2. If Scripture has such an important role in the development of our understanding of Christian doctrine and in helping us to live God's way, how can we effectively 'tap into' this resource (pp38-41)?

3. Focusing on the truth revealed in Scripture stops us from turning aside "to myths" (p42). What are the main "myths" that can beguile us today?

4. Consider the picture of the unashamed workman (pp43-44). What are the main ideas of the work in your life that will meet the Lord's scrutiny?

Fight the Good Fight

Timothy had been told that he had to make sure that his analysis and presentation of the Word of Truth was authentic and careful, so that the message would not be distorted, either by carelessness, or because he had been influenced by the heretics with their high-sounding ideas. He had to steer a straight course through all the maze of ideas. That would not be easy. It would require care and attention to what he believed, and discipline in his thinking. But Timothy was also required to maintain a Christ-like attitude towards people in the face of provocation, opposition and abuse, and that would not be easy either. It would require discipline in the way he reacted and behaved, and it would require self-control.

Fight the good fight

And this need for discipline and self-control in belief and in practice leads us to the final aspect of Timothy as *Man of God*, the command to "Fight the good fight". The first passage where Timothy is addressed as "*Man of God*" is in 1 Timothy 6.

> But you, *Man of God*, flee from all this....Fight the good fight of the faith. Take hold of the eternal life to which you were called when you made your good confession in the presence of many witnesses. In the sight of God, who gives life to everything, and of Christ Jesus, who while testifying before Pontius Pilate made the good confession, I charge you to keep this commandment without spot or blame until the appearing of our Lord Jesus Christ. (1 Timothy 6:11-14)

We cannot avoid being struck by the seriousness with which Paul makes this point to Timothy, but what is he actually asking Timothy to do? First of all, the metaphor is not one of aggression. It is one of endurance, perseverance and training. The verb used here (and the noun that goes with it: "Fight the good *fight*") indicates not a military picture so much as a sporting one. It means to contend for a prize, and this is usually taken as referring to the Olympic Games. The tense of the verb also indicates a continuous process rather than a one-off. Now Paul, of course, was very fond of analogies from sport. For example, in 1 Timothy 4:7-8, we read:

> Have nothing to do with godless myths and old wives tales; rather, *train yourself* to be godly.

For the *Man of God*, life is a continual disciplined struggle in this sense, and he has to keep in training constantly so that when the opportunity for testing comes, he will be ready and able to challenge in the race, and the goal that is in mind is eternal life (1 Timothy 6:12), which Paul tells Timothy to seize hold of. The tense of the verb in this verse suggests a once and for all act. However, this is a passage that can cause confusion, because eternal life is not offered in Scripture as a reward for work done, because salvation is by grace through faith. By mentioning it as a prize, there is an implication that some people whose service is flawed, but whose faith is genuine will not win it.

So what idea is Paul trying to put over by this picture of reaching out and grabbing the prize? It appears to be simply this; that although salvation is not by works, the Christian who takes his faith seriously will try to work through his faith and live out the implications of it on a daily basis (Philippians 2:12). He will set his mind on things above where Christ is seated rather than on earthly things, because he is now raised with Christ. His whole reach is upward to grasp hold of the eternal life that comes to him in Christ.

Timothy had been called by God, and he had accepted that call in the presence of many witnesses. It is not entirely clear whether Paul is referring to Timothy's conversion or his ordination, when God called him to a particular work. So Paul urges Timothy here to discipline himself like an athlete, get in training for godliness, that he might go on and win the prize of the games.

War the good warfare

Although the metaphor in 1 Timothy 6 does not appear to be a military one, the second passage in this connection does contain a military picture.

> Timothy, my son, I give you this instruction in keeping with the

prophecies once made about you, so that by following them you may fight the good fight, holding on to faith and a good conscience. (1 Timothy 1:18-19)

There are a number of similarities between this passage and 1 Timothy 6: the solemn instruction, the reference to prophecies about Timothy (which we know from 1 Timothy 4:14 were made at the time of his ordination) and the exhortation to fight the good fight. But "fight the good fight" is a different Greek phrase altogether from 1 Timothy 6. It is literally "war the good warfare". So this is a military picture. Again this is a popular picture with Paul. The armour of God in Ephesians is the obvious example, with different parts of the soldier's armour corresponding to the protection given by the Lord. The Christian is to wear this protection to give him security and make him an effective soldier. If he does not wear his armour, he will falter. Paul sees the Christian life as a war; a constant battle against sin within us and Satan-inspired attacks from outside. Paul mentions these two aspects in 2 Corinthians 10:5 where he speaks of opposing attacks from outside in terms of "demolishing arguments and every pretension that sets itself up against the knowledge of God", and subduing inner temptations in terms of "taking captive every thought to make it obedient to Christ".

But how was Timothy to fight this good fight? The *NIV* says "by following" the prophecies made about him, which is possibly not the best rendering. It is really "according to the prophecies" and the sense would appear to be "braced by them" (Kelly p57). Statements (presumably inspired) were made about Timothy. They may have been declarations of his character or of what God was going to accomplish through him. Here, Paul calls on Timothy to remember them, so that he can take encouragement and strength from them.

These prophecies appear to have been at his ordination, and, as we saw in 1 Timothy 6 above, Paul also mentions Timothy's confession, which also would appear to be at the same time. From one or two comments Paul makes, there is a suggestion that Timothy was a rather sensitive individual who tended not to be assertive, and who would therefore not find it easy to be in charge of a church where there were so many aggressive heretics in the congregation. So Paul says to Timothy:

- Remember you are a soldier in a war, so you must war a good warfare. Stand firm against attacks from outside and negative thoughts from inside. Wear your armour.
- When you were ordained a number of prophecies were made about you, your potential and what you would accomplish.
- Therefore, with that encouragement, go for it. Don't give up or lower your guard.

But although we cannot tell what exactly the prophecies were, we do know the two areas that Paul was concerned about—holding on to faith and a good conscience (1 Timothy 1:19).

We have earlier considered the two aspects to the pursuit of godliness—the vertical aspect of faith towards God and the horizontal aspect of our dealings with others. The two are inseparable; godliness being likeness to Christ lived out on a daily basis. The active conscience plays a major role in the outworking of our faith on a daily basis. "The purity of one's faith is directly related to the effectiveness of one's conscience" (Towner p59). And the need for real faith and an active conscience keeps recurring. For example, elsewhere in 1 Timothy we read:

> The goal of this command is love, which comes from a pure heart
> and a good conscience and a sincere faith. (1 Timothy 1:5)

> They (deacons) must keep hold of the deep truths of the faith with
> a clear conscience. (1 Timothy 3:9)

Such teachings (things taught by demons) come through hypocritical liars, whose consciences have been seared as with a hot iron. (1 Timothy 4:2)

Here in 1 Timothy 1:19 also, Paul shows what happens when someone "rejects" conscience. The *NIV* suggests that it is both faith and conscience that are being rejected. However, Moffatt, in his translation, and a number of commentators point out that the passage refers to the conscience only being "rejected", which is very thought-provoking. It also makes sense, because if you are "rejecting" your faith, it seems a bit pointless to say immediately that you will make shipwreck of your faith, as Paul does in the second half of verse 19. That would be rather obvious. It is the rejection of the *conscience* that causes the shipwreck of our faith.

"Rejecting" is a positive putting away, rather than neglect, and rejection of the work of conscience will eventually affect faith. While we can understand that if we have errors in our belief they will have a knock-on effect on the way we live, it is also true that if we insist on behaving in a particular wrong way, that can have a negative influence on our faith. Frequently loss of faith by Christians is caused not by persuasive arguments leading to a rejection of faith, but by the determination to behave in a way that is contrary to God's revealed will for His people.

So Timothy has to war a good warfare, which has the dual aspect of having a genuine faith (see 2 Timothy 1:5), and keeping his conscience active so that he does not fall into traps of wrong behaviour, which can "shipwreck" his faith. And throughout 1 and 2 Timothy the message is constantly repeated that Timothy has to be on the alert all the time. He is a soldier on duty. And there are various passages in the two epistles where Paul uses verbs that suggest the need for discipline and endurance.

Be diligent in these matters....*Watch* your life and doctrine closely. *Persevere* in them. (1 Timothy 4:15-16)

Guard what has been entrusted to your care. (1 Timothy 6:20)

Guard the good deposit that was entrusted to you—*guard* it with the help of the Holy Spirit who lives in us. (2 Timothy 1:14)

The soldier, the athlete and the farmer

Paul has used the metaphors of the Christian as athlete and as soldier to encourage Timothy to persevere in the pursuit of godliness, to keep going and not to lose sight of the fact that he must discipline himself at all times.

- He is an athlete in training, so he cannot relax or he may not win the prize.
- He is a soldier in warfare, so he cannot relax or the enemy will penetrate his armour.

But in 2 Timothy 2:3-7 Paul combines the two pictures of soldier and athlete, and adds a third, that of the farmer.

Endure hardship with us like a good soldier of Christ Jesus. No one serving as a soldier gets involved in civilian affairs—he wants to please his commanding officer. Similarly, if anyone competes as an athlete, he does not receive the victor's crown unless he competes according to the rules. The hardworking farmer should be the first to receive a share of the crops. Reflect on what I am saying, for the Lord will give you insight into all this.

"Endure hardship" really fails to bring out the full sense of the word, which means "Take your share in our suffering". The same word is used in 2 Timothy 1:8, "Join with me in suffering for the gospel." Soldiers are expected to suffer while they are on active duty. It is hardly surprising, and Paul uses the comparison directly in 2 Timothy 2:3.

Paul was about to come to the end of his ministry, but the torch had to be picked up by others, and he wanted Timothy, as a Christian leader, to understand the fact that he was going to experience persecution and serious opposition. And he sees the suffering that Timothy was about to share in as being part of his own suffering. But it is not only Christian leaders who are facing this difficulty.

In fact, everyone who wants to live a godly life in Christ Jesus will be persecuted. (2 Timothy 3:12)

So what Paul has to say to Timothy, as church leader and *Man of God*, is equally applicable to any of us who aspire to be *men and women of God*. Paul, then, gives Timothy this threefold picture of a soldier, an athlete and a farmer. There are, however, some differences between them.

The soldier: The soldier does not entangle himself in civilian affairs, no matter how legitimate these may be, because his sole aim is to please his commanding officer. This is one of the most striking images for the Christian who really wants to live out his/her faith. Everything else, apart from the service of the Lord, is of secondary importance. From the soldier Timothy learns single-mindedness and, in verse 3, endurance.

The athlete: The athlete can only be crowned if he keeps to the rules. These rules in the Olympics of old, extended not only to the race, but to the training. Athletes had to declare on oath that they had fulfilled ten months training (Guthrie p141). If they had not done the training they could not be crowned. From the athlete Timothy learns self-discipline.

The farmer: The emphasis in this verse is on the word "hardworking". It is the hardworking farmer rather than the slacker, who will reap the rewards and who is entitled to receive the first of the crops. From the farmer Timothy learns perseverance—how to go on doing backbreaking work faithfully when nothing much seems to be happening.

Although there are therefore slightly different aspects to the picture, the three examples come together in one common theme: each man is looking beyond the immediate present to the greater benefit that will follow. The soldier disregards the sufferings of the present in order to win the commendation of his commanding officer in the future. The athlete disciplines himself and keeps to the rules in order that he may win the prize at the end of the race. The farmer works hard throughout the year in order to reap the benefits at the future harvest. They all look beyond the present difficulty to the future glory and realise that the pain and hard work now is worthwhile because it is outweighed by the joy and the rewards that will be there at the end. This, of course, is what Paul says in so many words in Romans 8:18 and also in 2 Corinthians 4:17.

> I consider that our present sufferings are not worth comparing with the glory that will be revealed in us. (Romans 8:18)

> For our light and momentary troubles are achieving for us an eternal glory that far outweighs them all. (2 Corinthians 4:17)

And when Paul pulls all this together in verses 8-10 of 2 Timothy 2, he follows his common practice of using himself as an example.

> Remember Jesus Christ, raised from the dead, descended from David. This is my gospel, for which I am suffering even to the point of being chained like a criminal. But God's word is not chained. Therefore I endure everything for the sake of the elect, that they too may obtain the salvation that is in Christ Jesus, with eternal glory. (2 Timothy 2:8-10)

His opening statement is extremely striking. It is not so much the *fact* that

Jesus Christ was raised from the dead that Timothy is asked to remember, but the risen, living Jesus Christ, drawing attention to a present experience of the living Lord. The one who came to earth, descended through David's line, is alive and actively involved in the life of His people. Paul emphasises the fact that these sentiments are consistent with his gospel, and, having encouraged Timothy to suffering and endurance, he cites himself as an example.

In 2 Timothy 2:3 he has said "Endure hardship *with us*". Here in verse 9 he gives one example of his own suffering—suffering to the point of being chained as a criminal. In 2 Timothy 2:3 he has urged Timothy to "endure". In verse 10 he says, "Therefore (i.e. because God's Word cannot be chained and goes out doing its work), for that reason, I endure everything for the sake of the elect."

Paul was Timothy's great example. He has just spurred Timothy on to endure to the end, because of the glory that is to come. Now he demonstrates the priorities of his own thinking in that direction. And again, as in Romans 8 and 2 Corinthians 4, he speaks of eternal glory, at the end of verse 10, but these glories are not just for himself. Part of the glory for him is seeing the salvation and glorification of other believers, and that salvation is only possible through Christ, to those who are "in Christ".

So Paul wants Timothy to be like a good soldier, suffering without backing down, and enduring hardship. He wants him to discipline himself, like an Olympic athlete, submitting to daily training to build himself up, growing in grace and godliness so that, like an athlete who keeps to the rules, he will be eligible to win the prize.

The finishing line for Paul

In this chapter we see Paul using himself as an example to Timothy, speaking of his own suffering and endurance. But Paul's need for suffering and endurance is about to end. We have seen the places where he has told Timothy to "fight the good fight" and "war the good warfare". And in 2 Timothy 4:6-8 he uses that metaphor for himself.

> For I am already being poured out like a drink offering, and the time has come for my departure. I have fought the good fight, I

have finished the race, I have kept the faith. Now there is in store for me the crown of righteousness, which the Lord, the righteous judge, will award to me on that day—and not only to me, but also to all who have longed for his appearing.

Here in verse 7 Paul uses the same phrase for himself that he used for Timothy in 1 Timothy 6, "I have struggled the good struggle", and again the metaphor seems more sporting than military. This is confirmed by the next phrase, "I have finished the race". Then in plain speech, "I have kept the faith". Paul repeatedly urged Timothy to "guard the deposit of truth" which he had been given, and:

- not to be corrupted by false teaching, but
- to stick to the pattern of teaching Paul and others had given him, and
- to stick to the teaching of Scripture.

Now Paul can say of himself that he kept the faith. That is what he wants Timothy to do also.

In the Christian "race", Paul has said that the "athlete" cannot win unless he sticks to the rules for training, and the rules for the race. But here the picture of the race breaks down, because in the race, or any sporting event, there is only one winner. For the others, who may have given everything, there is only despair and dejection. But that is not the case in the Christian race. Notice that Paul says here "I have *finished* the race". Not "won" the race: only to finish it. That is enough, and what lies ahead? The crown of righteousness, which the Lord will give to *all* who have longed for His appearing. There is not *one* winner in the Christian race. The prize is on offer to *all* who finish the course and keep the faith.

Paul has been stressing to Timothy the need for discipline, endurance, perseverance and the ability to cope with suffering. He is to fight the good fight, which has a double aspect. First, there is a need to hold on to the true faith using, as a pattern, the message passed on to him by Paul and others, based on Scripture. In other words, he is to preserve the apostolic message intact. But secondly he must keep a good conscience, pursuing godliness with a consistent lifestyle, constantly measuring his practice against his beliefs and making sure that his beliefs are worked out in practice. By doing this he will reach up to take hold of the prize and be an effective *Man of God* in Ephesus.

And what is the prize here in chapter 4? The prize is again reminiscent of the games, where the laurel wreath was presented to the successful athlete. Paul describes it here as the "crown of righteousness", that is, the crown that is the reward given to the righteous man. The qualification for receiving such a crown is given in verse 8: it is offered to "all who have longed for his appearing". To those who live as *men and women of God* in the world, with their eyes fixed on the things that are above, and who live in anticipation of the return of Christ, this special crown is offered.

Questions for discussion and meditation

1. Paul encourages Timothy to discipline himself like an athlete in training for the games (pp51-53). Think through the areas in your own life where such training is required.

2. In 1 Timothy 1:19 Paul suggests that the rejection of conscience can cause the shipwreck of our faith (pp 50-51). How does this happen? How can it be prevented?

3. Timothy is compared with a soldier in 2 Timothy 2:3-4. A good soldier does not get involved in "civilian affairs". What does Paul mean when he warns Timothy not to become involved in "civilian affairs"?

4. In 2 Timothy 4 Paul, in effect, writes his own epitaph. If you had the chance to do the same, what would you like to be able to write? What work of God needs to be done to make it so?

Conclusion: A Blueprint for the *Man of God*

In Romans 8:29, Paul states that those whom God foreknew He predestined to be conformed to the likeness of His Son. If we want to be *men and women of God*, as we recognise that this is our destiny, we should see the implications for our present lives. These should be characterised by godliness, with its double aspect of bringing our mindset into line with that of the Lord Jesus Christ and developing a consistency between our framework of belief and our behaviour. For the Christian, seeking after godliness is not an optional extra, but the logical outcome of our relationship with God in Christ.

Firstly, the religion of the natural man should be rejected. Unregenerate man down through the ages has developed religious practices designed to build up merit for himself for the afterlife, or to persuade a hostile or fickle deity to give him blessings in the present. By contrast, the *Man of God* knows that he cannot put God into his debt and that all he receives from God comes by His grace through faith. The recognition of this fact gives the Christian a motivation to serve that is unique. The reason for the pursuit of godliness is a response to the work of God in Christ, who has qualified him to share in the inheritance of the saints in the kingdom of light (Colossians 1:12).

Paul also variously describes human religion in terms of "godless myths", "false doctrines", "godless chatter" and "what is falsely called knowledge". The imagery here suggests metaphysical speculation not rooted in any form of reality, but claiming a special knowledge available only to initiates. This error later manifested itself in gnosticism and today has its counterpart in some aspects of the New Age movement. Paul's antidote to false religion is training in godliness. The seared conscience of the heretics is set in contrast to the active conscience that a Christian should possess, helping him to achieve consistency between his belief system and his daily lifestyle. Our vertical relationship with God in terms of our knowledge of Him and His purposes needs to be worked out in our daily conduct. This working out involves a strategic decision on our part to turn our backs on the ways of the world and to embrace God's way.

Secondly, and following on from the consideration of the religious realm, we must turn our backs on the unhelpful influences and the prevailing philosophies of the pagan society in which we live, with its materialism and its domination by selfish passions and desires. Instead we should dedicate ourselves to the pursuit of the qualities that Paul has described as characterising the *Man of God*: moral uprightness of character, underpinned by the inner strengths of faith and endurance. This is something that is particularly difficult as we are all children of our culture and it is hard to avoid absorbing the outlook of those around us. These characteristics indicated by Paul represent the balanced Christian life, with what we believe directly affecting the type of people we are, and this, in turn, feeding into the gentle way that we relate to others. In other words, there is complete consistency between our beliefs, our nature and our conduct. The attitudes that we display towards others should be very different from those of the world.

Therefore, as a third issue, the attitudes of the man of the world should also have no place in the lifestyle of the Christian. Paul is thinking primarily of the situation of Timothy the church leader, dealing with heretics and unbelievers with whom he comes in contact in evangelistic or pastoral work. For those of us who are not involved "professionally" in this, it has application in the first instance to the way we approach those we encounter as we witness for the Lord, and with whom we discuss our faith. Ultimately, though, it relates to all aspects of our dealings with others. Paul states that the approach of the worldly person, with his love of argument and quarrelling over trivia should be avoided. Such an outlook generates an atmosphere of anger and resentment and, in addition, can have a negative effect on the faith of others. For these two reasons the *Man of God* must try to avoid foolish speculations and remain reasonable and gentle in the face of provocation. His prime motive must be the building up of the other, whether this is with a view to that person's salvation, instruction or restoration, and that is more difficult in an atmosphere of hostility.

Paul paints a somewhat bleak picture of the degeneration that will take place "in the last days", with growing ignorance of the truth of God, and an increase in deception. The solution for Timothy and us is to have a thorough understanding of the Word of God. The religious framework of the *Man of God* is based on the revelation that God has given of Himself and His purposes in the inspired Scriptures. It is only by rooting our faith firmly in the teaching of Scripture that we can be sure that we do not believe error.

Our understanding of Scripture, like Timothy's, may come from a number of sources—our own personal meditation, the reading of commentaries and other works by other *men and women of God,* or discussion with individuals whose knowledge and judgment is greater than ours. Whatever the source of our information, it must be compared with our reference point, the teaching of the Word of God. The Scriptures alone, understood through the work of the Revealer of God's truth—the Holy Spirit, can give us the understanding that leads to salvation, and thereafter be used for guiding us in relation to both our doctrine and our conduct, so that the *Man of God* may be thoroughly equipped for every good work (2 Timothy 3:17).

This, then, is the pursuit of godliness, and there is no easy route to it. Paul tells us that it requires *training.* Godliness with contentment is great gain, but that contentment is something he *learned.* Righteousness is something to be *pursued.* Paul gives us some insight into the application required for this task with his threefold metaphor of the soldier, the athlete and the farmer. The soldier dedicates himself to pleasing his commanding officer and allows himself no distractions from the task. The athlete disciplines himself and keeps to the rules to win the prize at the games. The farmer is prepared to continue doing hard work over a long period of time for the sake of the crop to be reaped at the coming harvest. The teaching for the *Man of God* is clear: he needs the strength to endure hardship in the present for the sake of the infinitely greater glory that will follow in the future.

We have to face up to our obligations as believers in the world. We have been raised with Christ and our lives are now hidden with Christ in God (Colossians 3:1-3). We must therefore try to live in a manner that is appropriate to who we are and to behave in a way that is worthy of our calling. The decision to forsake the way of the world and to follow the way of Christ is no more than the logical outworking of our faith.

But it is extremely difficult for us, with our fallen nature, to do this. It requires dedication and consistent application and can take a lifetime to work through. Thankfully, however, we are not left completely to our own devices. Paul had learned the hard lesson of how to be content irrespective of the situation in which he found himself. However, his confidence and strength was not his own. In Philippians 4:13 he points out the secret of his success:

I can do everything through him who gives me strength.

That strength is available to us also, two thousand years later, as we try to walk in the footsteps of Paul and Timothy, as *men and women of God*.

References

Allen, Stuart. *Letters from Prison*, The Berean Publishing Trust
The Economist. *Jesus – Obituary*. April 3rd 1999, p101
Green, Michael. *2 Peter and Jude*, Tyndale New Testament Commentary (Revised Edition)
Guthrie, Donald. *The Pastoral Epistles*, Tyndale New Testament Commentary
Hanson, Anthony Tyrrell. *The Pastoral Letters*, The Cambridge Bible Commentary on the New English Bible
Kelly, JND. *A Commentary on the Pastoral Epistles 1 & 2 Timothy, Titus*, Black's New Testament Commentaries
Macleod, Donald. *A Faith to Live By. Studies in Christian Doctrine*, Mentor Publications
Towner, Philip H. *1-2 Timothy & Titus*, The IVP New Testament Commentary Series
Welch, Charles H. *An Alphabetical Analysis, Vol. 2*, The Berean Publishing Trust